D0645481

Love Catalogue: Book I
Poems for 101 Varieties of Love
ISBN 978-0-578-58357-0
ISBN-13 978-0-578-58357-0
by JV Connors
Copyright 2019
First edition, edited, hoping to find an agent /
publisher
Interpersonal Peace Center
Silver City, NM

Contents

*This book is dedicated to my therapy clients
(from 1974 to the present), who have taught me
so much about love's work in their painful
soul-searching with me. I pray all of them have
found and will find happiness and peace.*

Chapter 1: Innate Love

But that I know, love is begun by time,
And that I see, in passages of proof,
Time qualifies the spark and fire of it.
William Shakespeare (King Claudius
speaking), Hamlet, Act 4, Scene 7, (1602)

Universe Love

All of us and everything, began
within a white-hot subatomic spark, that,
fourteen billion years ago,
expanded to the size of galaxies in an instant,
then cooled into halos of darkness
that birthed all the seeds of the universe.

Inside those burning primordial plasmas,
those first elements cooled, crashed,
exploded and scattered, but gradually
gravity, and something much larger,
that we cannot see or understand,
took hold and pulled the ethers together
into stars, planets,
and eventually, life-forms.

The universe is still expanding
and tearing itself apart,
constantly destroying old patterns and forms,
but it is also guided by healing powers
that bring together the pieces left behind.

Love may have begun with those invisible
hands,
gathering our scattered remains
and healing us, millions of times,
to dance into a new universe
and make it beautiful.

Baby Love

As babies we feel loved
by adoring faces, soft voices,
gentle nurturing and unguarded openness.

Parent and child are drawn deep
savoring each other's fragrant love energy,
surrendering with complete trust
into that affectionate delight.

The first bond is irresistible and timeless,
for most there is no question
that we belong together,

That primal bond has guided human evolution,
uniting us as families and communities,
inspiring many sacred laws
and shaping our enjoyment of life's gifts.

Each of us has known some degree
of this fundamental belonging and trust,
where there is no reason for fear,
fighting, wounding or rejection.

Children's Love

Is luminous and open-hearted,
with a musical lightness
that can melt frozen adult thinking
and bring a pleasant pang to older souls
watching their play.

Too many adults have a 10-foot wall
between their awareness
and children's experiences,
having pushed their own child-self
deeply underground
for many imaginable reasons.

Still these babies continually
soften most every one
of our hard hearts
with their open smiles and questions,
their songs and silly stories

Transforming us
into playful friends,
kind people,
protectors and heroes.

Young Love

Is passionate, impulsive,
driven by hormones,
sex-obsessed, aching,
caressing, feeling under clothes,
giving into passions,
hating being apart.

Young lovers adore
their projected visions of each other,
and savor every moment
of their gratifying connection.

Young love is vibrant,
playful, mischievous, adventurous,
shouts its feelings,
and wants to conquer all obstacles,

But its idealism often crumbles
when faced with ordinary troubles
and frustration takes over.

When passion fades, young lovers
may impulsively do something cruel
to break their lover's heart,
or, become stupid, stinky, or careless.

The young may even throw lovers in the trash
and hook up with danger
in their fever to avoid
love's pain.

Chapter 2: Love Mirages

*Don't look for big things, just do small things
with great love.*
Mother Teresa, *Come Be My Light* (2009)

Nice Love

Many were taught as children to be quiet,
pleasant, agreeable,
to never challenge or make trouble,
to never demand attention,
and always take care of others first.

So, we learned to please others,
to work hard for approval.

And became so focused on gratifying others
that we develop little blood or muscle
to stand up for our own needs
or for the common good,

Frequently putting up with careless stupidity
and reckless aggression
until we are completely overwhelmed.

And when we make that rude discovery,
that all do not live by the rules of nice,
our nice love turns into a pale shell,
still pretty,
but crumbling at
the first *ping*.

Fairy Tale Love

Many of us absorbed ideals of *true* love
from the gorgeous visions
of childhood fairy tales--

Our lovers will be breathtaking
with perfect skin and teeth,
a beautiful voice,
lush hair,
and a flawless body.

They're always clean and
their breath never stinks.

They will have numerous tricks for getting out of
trouble,
and magic will be their ally.

Their love will complete us,
take care of us,
rescue and protect us,
never leave us.

Ahhhh,
what pleasure it will be
to find such fulfilling perfection
in the person designed
to be our soul mate!

We dream and wait.

Romantic Love

Sweet, creamy and delicious,
so enticing and addictive,
a perfect treasure.

The tantalizing sugar of romance,
lures us into the sport
of hunting for a partner,

Using the delightful art
of sexual enticement, as advertised,
to find a romance target,
and sometimes it works,
if we can stand the humiliation.

This quest is aided
by an irresistible, beautiful fog
that makes us see pathetic fools as movie stars
we should chase and adore
while we overlook good hearts
who don't fit market criteria.

So much is given up
hunting for that ethereal prize--
forgetting work, art, other loved ones,
and so many things that really matter.

And there's no guarantee that we will score,
or ultimately like the love object we capture,
or, we might get dumped
for not fulfilling their fantasies.

How can two good people find lasting love
together
or grow a loving family,
through such a brutal sport
in an idiots' maze?

Love's Happy Ending

The search for happily ever after
lures us
with images of ultimate contentment,
sunsets, cascading waters and cozy vistas
accompanied by sweet music.

The ultimate fix for all of our ills--
the illusion of completeness.

Loneliness and grief will be overcome
as we reach that place of serenity
and find the welcoming shelter
of our beloved's arms.

We long to realize these visions,
seldom satisfied
with our present circumstances,

And miss noticing
the gentle streams of warmth
that surround us from many sources.

Screen Love

Is such a beautiful fabrication,
a pretend paradise
that sucks all of our dreamings
into the garbage of babble,
or, turns them into poison.

With a wide menu of luscious illusions
available to titillate
every one of our desires
(in such a variety of configurations!),
so we are sure to lose our grip.

All to feed off of our life-juice,
and tell us who to be,
what to strive for,
how to spend our time and money,
what to shun and despise,
and who or what to punish.

Screen love holds the keys
to social control,
and despises those who question it.

Dualistic Love

Is low effort and simple--
yes or no,
because it's survival based--
safe or not.

We adore you,
you are pure perfection,
and your imperfections have such symmetry,
they make you more perfect.

Or, *we're repelled by you,*
you are monstrous,
cruel and calculating,
a hateful being
who causes all our misery.

Dualistic love gives us terrible choices--
love unconditionally,
or hate and shun,
marking our categories with deep lines,
and blurring out everything in between.

Then, those who are "bad"
(in our opinion)
fall out of the haven of our concern,
become ugly
(abuse-worthy),
and disappear
(to us).

While those of us in the good box
must strain and stress to stay there,
ultimately forgetting our principles
or shaping them to please manipulators
with increasingly more powerful rationalizations.

When we only see the shiny side
of what we deem acceptable,
life becomes very small.

Chapter 3: Love Misadventures

Love is the ultimate outlaw. It just won't adhere to any rules. The most any of us can do is to sign on as its accomplice. Instead of vowing to honor and obey, maybe we should swear to aid and abet. That would mean that security is out of the question.

Tim Robbins (Bernard to Leigh-Cheri, Ch. 46), *Still Life with Woodpecker* (1980)

Love Drama

Drama is a chaos spewing cyclone
that uproots us
and throws us against each other,
turning everyday fools into lovers
and enemies.

We take on roles in each other's storylines,
strutting around our common spaces,
and breathe honey and fire towards each other,
exhilarated to struggle, dance, amuse and fall
as we enact our pointless tales.

When we find ourselves falling into
the childish logic of drama,
we become 'victim' to the other's 'wrongdoer',
feeding each other doubt and blame,
fueled by desire and high adrenaline.

Mistakes and flaws can become intolerable,
then targeted for nailing--

You spent how much?
Don't make us late again!
You make my life such misery!

Then we question, twist and judge others'
choices, gifts and dreams
and remain clueless to the power that gives
away
to create our own fulfillment.

And if we get sucked into drama's coercive lie
that we have no fault,
a blame war may erupt
and savage for years.

Drama brings conflict, charged anger,
and discontentment with our lot,

Distorts petty mistakes,
projects bad intentions,

Destroys relationships, families, workplaces
and communities,

But somehow it works.

These crazy exchanges of desire and blame
intrigue us enough
to keep us connecting,
and stimulate our systems
of reproduction, verbal expression,
art, science and adventure.

Drama is the expressive and colorful way
we tell our stories worldwide,
but it brings so much suffering.

Perhaps we'll find a better way
someday.

Addicted Love

In the glow of inebriation,
many become infatuated with golden dreams
and declare love to a user companion,
even committing to lifelong attachment
with someone who compels
through that glorious haze.

When we are addicted to drugs or alcohol,
we cannot love
because all we know is need
for our escape of choice,
letting it dominate every aspect of our lives,
and blind us to people's hearts.

Some addicts have too much injury to love
and become predatory,
using and abusing family, friends and lovers,
even stealing from their own children,
constantly excusing their own cruelty.

We so want to love and be loved,
we want it to be real
and take the pretty illusions seen when high
as reliable (self-serving) truth,
like children do.

It is easy to imagine there's love
within the warm pleasure and release
that come from mind-altering substances,
but, it is a trap

that may turn life into a nightmare
and abandon us far from home.

Food Love

Food is the ultimate nurturer of body
from a mothering earth,

As food caresses, kisses,
delights the senses,
teases, excites, pleasures and satisfies
leaving the belly happy,

And it is a vehicle for love--
conveying nurturing and affection
to children, friends and family
over thousands of years.

Sharing meals with neighbors and coworkers
builds community spirit, friendliness
and mutual concern,
while bringing food to those suffering
comforts them and aids their healing.

Food supports our weary efforts
like a good lover should
but does not demand more than its due
because it adapts to our timing
(if it does not spoil),

Trouble comes if food becomes a substitute for
love,
feeding the hungers of loneliness
and stroking petulant egos.

Still, food is far less complicated and more
reliable
than words or actions between people who love,
because it satisfies
when people are too dangerous,
or words are frozen inside.

Love Online

Is not troubled by physical reality,
nor limited by distance, age or class.

We can be our best selves virtually,
quite attractive, dynamic and wise.

Trust is easily given there,
with little to risk,
it's only when we meet away from that shining
realm,
that our yucky habits and flaws
may reveal themselves.

While in this domain of ideas,
without the demands of time and substance,
we can be the best lovers, mentors and friends,
supporting, advising and truth telling.

Many of us feel safe enough
in that controlled world
to listen,
and let in their concerns,
so we can be our best.

We are freer there
to share ideas and stories,
to be respectful,
to use words constructively,
and to quell the seeds of hate
towards each other.

Even in our age of brutality,
many forms of dialogue and peace-building
can be found there
(along with vast idiocies).

Good people could prevail
out in that field of energy strings
(if not overwhelmed by market forces
or contrary trolls),
to help us reach our potential
for balance and peace.

Traveling Love

Is whimsical and unpredictable,
courageous and fragile,
and usually worth the risk.

We may collide with complete strangers
and start talking in odd places--
stuck in line together,
seated nearby on a bus or train,
or browsing at the market,
then something sweet may emerge.

In the constantly changing chaos and danger
of wandering from place to place
a person with common viewpoints is gold,
bringing sweet company,
useful information, feedback,
safety, and comfort.

Sometimes passion evolves,
with or without expectations.

The question of what is real
is always under the surface,
unanswerable, until the trip is over
and long in the past.

Smoker's Love

Behind their smoggy veil,
there is a unique culture,
a unity of spirit,
mysteriously lurking.

Savoring the beauty of smoke
(their loving fortress),
they enjoy their freedom
with humor and
more quiet than you find most places.

From their dark refuge
they lose sight of the pressures
and the snide looks,
to enjoy their kinky camaraderie.

Though separated from the outer world,
they feel their judgments
gnawing away inside.

Back Door Love

What does it mean when
we won't acknowledge our lovers
in front of others?

When family and friends
don't know who we are sleeping with?

We might question our motivation
as they slip in and out the back.

Are we hiding
from family pressures,
community class snobbery,
religious prohibitions or racial biases?

Are we ashamed of them
because they are poor or uneducated,
a drinking or drugging buddy,
an injured soul we took pity on?

Are we protecting our own reputation
and just using them
because one of us is committed to another,
or they are much older or younger,
or one of us has a social position
to protect?

We might reconsider our reasons
before using the back door,
because it can stain our memories
with shame.

Skunk Love

Love can become quite smelly
when we don't think
and fall into someone's bed
because we're horny or needy.

If we don't love or respect
the person we are sleeping with
we gradually start to stink
from half-truthing and using.

After rolling in that mucky energy,
the stench of compromising sex
sticks to our skin,
and exudes from our pores,
then it pollutes other areas of our lives,
relationships, work,
even spirituality,
with foulness.

It takes years for that stink to wear off,
but self-reckoning
and risky, humble honesty,
may help us to stop using people
and feel clean again.

Rock Love

Is sturdy, steady,
and so secure,
reliable, deeply comforting
and heavy.

Rock love is always there,
giving us faith and strength,
as long as nothing challenges it's hard logic.

Rock love can be oh so hard to change
because nothing and no one
can make it yield,
despite the constant batterings
of soft flesh falling against it,
trying to negotiate around
its rigid form.

Those whose paths cross with rock love
are often bruised deeply
and carry their resentments
in secret pouches.

Gorilla Love

Grabs us like a doll and squeezes.

We are the latest shiny toy
to entice and entertain
for a few minutes pleasure.

Many of us enjoy being swept away
by those primitive hands.

We willingly lay in the grass
and open our arms to enticing sociopaths,
forgetting who we are,
and not thinking what could happen
as we disregard all the rules.

The wildness of that lust and laughter
is supremely freeing and energizing,
while it lasts.

Gorilla love has no substance
though.

It takes us on a wild roller coaster ride,
and then stops
to look for another customer.

Forbidden Love

The power of denied wishes
creates a longing,
an obsession with whoever
we are told to stay away from.

This aching to taste what we desire
surges from our darkness,
climbing up our bones
and pressing on our brains.

Tantalizing images flood through,
our hands tingle and yearn to touch,
as the anticipation of pleasure
dominates our thoughts,

Blinding our minds to the truth
of whether this love is a good idea
or not.

Backwoods Love

Depends on the soil,
the hills, fields and woodlands,
and on the skills of survival.

Backwoods lovers knows the land intimately,
it's crevices, hiding places and secret treasures,
the animals and plants that provide food or
danger,
and the waterways that we see
and don't see.

Backwoods people live with constant sorrow--

The price of living on the land
is vulnerability to many harsh challenges,
demanding tremendous and brutal work
that often bears no fruit,
though time helps grow our understanding
of nature's contrary recipes,
so we can endure.

Backwoods lovers always help our neighbors,
for we need each other
to survive our common hardships,
and to celebrate our common joy.

We who love the wild lands
stay rooted through heartfelt community
gatherings,
music, prayer and celebrations,
and use them as antidotes

to the bitterness that poisons and shrivels
many of our companions.

Chapter 4: Destructive Love

*Every relationship of domination, of
exploitation, of oppression, is by definition
violent, whether or not the violence
is expressed by drastic means. In such
a relationship, dominator and dominated
alike are reduced to things - the former
dehumanized by an excess of power, the
latter by a lack of it. And things cannot love.*
Paulo Freire, *Pedagogy of the Oppressed*
(1968)

Money Love

We are deeply programmed to love money,
totally infatuated with its glittering illusions,
as money-lust messages press from all
directions
and become further rooted in our DNA,
so we have little chance of evading
money's addictive pull.

We crave money's decadent promises
and gorgeous gifts,
we love its power
to give us what we want,
go where we want,
and make others serve us happily.

Over time, money makes people fade away--
becoming shadows behind painted cardboard,
then we pose lovingly
with our paper beloveds.

Family, friends, even children, become things--
chess pieces of minor significance,
while possessions may be treasured above all
and become the basis for treachery
because money is the only thing that matters.

.

When people are not valued,
drugs, sex or danger
may become necessary to distract us
from our unbearable emptiness,

As we are sucked into money's all-consuming
vortex
of murderous decadence,
we find nothing survives
that matters.

Sexual Love

Sexual lust is mesmerizing
with drug-like hormones compelling us to believe
such easy, overwhelming bliss
is love.

Every touch is magic,
luring us to touch again,
to connect through hands, eyes, mouths...

Music rises as our spirits mingle,
we dance and play,
our voices harmonize,
while our minds indulge fantasies
of paradise.

Love takes time--
to explore the intersections of our complex
layers
and to work through life's challenges,
before we can actually live love
towards each other
and build a sheltering life together.

Sex may bring love, or not,
but we will not know what we reap
until we've endured the harsh road
of creating love's promises.

Selfish Love

We often want love to suit our needs
(sex, money, appearances, control, servitude...),
please our whims,
and meet our criteria,
without having to do the work
to honor our beloveds as people.

We don't care to see our lover's side,
to understand,
build trust,
accommodate, compromise,
reconcile differences,
or explore each other's hearts,
habits and troubles.

Our loving words may be meaningless,
when we don't consider what our lover needs,
or refuse to deal with their shadows.

If our lover is revealed
to not meet dream-lover criteria,
we often decide they are not worthy,
and turn our backs.

So much love is based on self-fulfilling
(delusional) stories,
only loving in convenience
and our commitment has less substance than
a trace of yesterday's dream.

Many of us are so self-serving
that we constantly walk away from
love's flesh and bones.

Love of Despair

If we give ourselves to despair,
we must remember that
it is a demanding partner,

Allowing no freedom for diversions,
fulfilling work,
or friends who do not console.

Others must wallow in the significance
of our sorrows,
and never question our enslavement
to this harsh master.

Despair constantly nags us,
focuses on what we don't have--
on disappointments,
slights against us,
and every wrong it can find
to feed its ravenous self-pity.

Friends and family who stick by us
gradually become unimportant,
other than their contributions to our misery
through their villainous hurts
or neglect of our pleading needs.

We will forget about love
as our time is spent in the service
of validating our tragic victimhood.

But we find darkness comforting

and the waves of pain that swallow us up
are a necessary price
for our comfortable, self-obsessed hole.

Angry Love

Is a stormy sea,
exhilarating, dark and dangerous.

When anger's fire ignites within love,
it becomes the master,
muffling love's voice
to serve anger's burning.

Angry lovers cannot hear each other
for anticipating each other's brutality
and the childish pleasure it brings.

Often we over-interpret little angers
until they grow huge
and self-righteously trample
the delicate strings between us
causing our music to become discordant
and harsh.

Angry love sabotages good will,
wearies care and trust,
destroys tenderness,
and sickens both
against compassion.

Brutal Love

Grows from the power of fear,
for both brutalizer and victim.

The passive needy one
thinks devoted sacrifice is love
and strives to answer doubts
with more pleasing.

The brutal needy one
thinks control and violence
are the price of love's security
for someone as broken as them.

The survival instinct drives both to stay
connected,
telling them to hold on so tightly
because disturbing threats arise
with the thought of letting go.

Anyone who questions this violent relationship,
can become the enemy to both,
for neither can fathom the possibility
of separation.

Years later, if they live,
loss, injury or fate
may break down the illusions
and bring one or both to realize
their legacy of pointless damage.

Predatory Love

There are many hungry loners
out in the wilderness
who scout shelter in the cold months
looking for some welcoming generous spirit
to share a little fat.

They track down the easy givers,
those who are wounded,
old or weak,
those seeking help to guard their caves
and willing to pay a price.

Then the control dance begins
giving and taking,
more, unoffered taking.

Family members will worry,
How much will they take?
and try to interfere,

But the wounded one will usually defend
the hungry heart in their keeping,
even as they suffer
from their callous disregard.

Friends hope for the best,
shake their heads, and wonder

How long
will this one last?

Malicious Love

Malicious people have given up on love,
they mock it like angry children,
and care not for their lovers,
only that they serve their desires.

These spiteful lovers do not really love,
but play the part of lover
for other motives.

They say what they don't mean
to temporarily enthrall,
judge others as not pleasing,
and coldly criticize every friend.

They ignore the cries of their beloveds
when they protest disregard and abuse,
or attack their credibility with lies,
always excusing their own rudeness.

Malicious lovers try to destroy love,
secretly despising the softness of innocents,
they draw them in,
disguised as sincere, giving eyes.

Chapter 5: Yucky Love

this love journey
is surely the hardest and
most twisted road I have taken
Rumi, translated by N. Khalili, *Rumi, dancing*
the flame **(13th Century / 2001)**

Hidden Love

So many of us are virtual strangers--
romantic partners, parents and children,
siblings, even lifelong friends,

Because we hide so much
from those we love,
what we really feel and think,
our deepest desires.

We say what we think they want to hear,
avoid touchy subjects,
and rarely speak the troubled feelings
burning beneath our smiles,

So many sweet declarations
are deceptions, as much to ourselves
as to any person we care for,
pretending to be someone
we think they will love.

When we say we love,
we might really mean –

I appreciate that you conform to my needs
enough
that I can stay with you.

or,

You are proof that I am adequate in my social
role

because you do not embarrass me in public
and you seldom give others reasons to gossip.

or,

I'm grateful that you accept my version of reality
and provide me with enough grounding
that I can face the world.

Spurred by such motivations,
we conceal our disappointments
and ignore issues that might rock the boat
or bring discomfort...

Even tender feelings,
appreciation and yearning to touch
are often silenced between
those together for a lifetime.

How strong can our love really be
if we don't talk,
and know so little
about what really happens inside
those we share our lives with?

Neglected Love

New love is wonderful,
exciting and life-changing.

Our lives blissfully revolve around each new
darling,
until time passes
and something new distracts our attention,
so our previous infatuation loses their pull.

Habit and time send a fog drifting over our
vision,
so we overlook faithful friends and lovers
for newly discovered faces and obsessions.

Then we take enduring beloveds for granted,
forget to nurture their spirits,
and become blind to their radiant grace.

Old love fades back into the shadows,
and even our most precious loves
become dull and gray
from neglect.

Lazy Love

In the course of most committed relationships,
there are testing times,
with too much stress
and things going wrong,
when our lover's needs deeply disturb,
and care may be forgotten.

The petty, childish ego takes over
and wants to get rid of the unpleasant,
having more and more
fantasies of escape.

Somewhere else, someone else,
would be clean,
would gratify our lacks
and desires.

This flawed relationship must be responsible
for our unhappiness,
having pushed our buttons too often.

Another road beckons.

Tired Love

We are so, so, overworked,
and exhausted from
obligations, demands, worries,
that never end
and become our way of life.

Every day is full of unpleasant drudgery,
leaving hardly any time for rest,
recharging,
or talking.

We wish so much
to be there for our beloveds,
but have so little energy,

That when we're together,
we forget how to connect
or to feel awe for sweet moments,
so we fake it.

Our flame is low
and sputtering,
our eyes fade
and colors turn gray.

Lost Love

So often, love fails
to overcome our impossible expectations.

We still criticize, dismiss, neglect,
focus on the negative,
and are blind to each other's inner struggles.

When we don't appreciate each other,
see the positive and say so,
relationships slowly dry up
and precious love slips away.

Years later, in a quiet moment,
we may remember their dear eyes,
the quiet bliss of their company,
and realize how much
we threw away.

Giving Love

We love to spoil our beloveds,
to delight them with gifts,
to please their senses,

But too many of us forget
that love needs balance,
and continue to give,
asking nothing in return,
so self-neglect becomes patterned.

Then we find ourselves bewildered
at the bottomless pit
of needs and wants
that keep demanding our time.

Still we push ourselves more,
forgetting that giving too much
makes us unattractive and annoying,
while making our gifts appear weak
and uninteresting.

Body Love (Fail)

We want delicious sex
without consequences,
and incredible melting flavors in our mouths
without indigestion or weight gain.

We expect slender bodies with perfect curves,
no lumps, and clear, tight skin.

We like to work or play late into the night,
forgetting rest,
filling our systems with chemicals
to feel relaxed or energized,
or to forget.

Sickness is an inconvenience
so we go to experts to fix or remove symptoms
with magical remedies.

We keep controlling and pushing
our flesh and bones
but don't want to hear body's meanings,
be aware of body's workings,
or understand body's problems,
so how can we take care of it?

When we act like we are divorced from our
bodies,
we live within them in stony opposition,
mind expecting obedience
and bewildered by body's rebellions.

How else can body say
that doesn't work for me,
but to make us suffer
or to send solemn ghosts into our future?

Gendered Love

Our binary male-female belief system
is an encyclopedia of insane rules
and conditions about gender
that imposes a horrendous cost on our lives
and our loving.

We are deeply conditioned to carry and enforce
the ancient social construct of gender,
for thousands of years
it has fundamentally dominated
how we evaluate and treat each other
as lovers, friends and family.

I. Manufactured Gender

Masculine and feminine roles are deeply
imprinted
through words and images a thousand times a
day,
while simultaneously we judge and are judged
for how we conform.

Conditioning us to squeeze ourselves
into gender's dualistic restrictions,
adopting limited social roles, bizarre costumes,
and unhealthy rituals
to be loved, or even accepted.

Then we are pressured to only seek partners
from the other side of the gender binary,

with fairy tales enticing our imaginations
while rejection fuels our nightmares.

II. Imprisoning Gender

This impossible gender script
becomes our predominant obsession about our
lives,
keeping us trapped in stories that never stop
or get better.

We must ignore other possibilities,
and all the evidence
that there are more than two choices of gender
and one choice for who to make a family with.

We must pretend not to notice how we don't fit,
how so many of us despair of trying
and suffer endlessly.

Society pays such a cost for our
judgmental genderism,
as we thrash each other constantly,
inflicting thousands of layers of damage,
with so much hatred
against we who push against our chains.

III. Gender Waking

Can we look for the blessings in difference?
In other ways of being and loving?
The amazing spectrum of appearances and life

patterns
so deep in character and history?

Can we acknowledge the many ways
of combining male and female and other?
Can we see the vivid beauty of differences?
Accept them
and let go of our fears?

There are many other genders around us
that take nothing from us
and do no damage.

IV. Gender Freedom

If we could let go of gender dualism rules,
break their heavy grip on our lives,
and stop playing the control game,

We could just be who we want to be,
dress and love as we like,

And free ourselves from so much useless strife,
work on the world's problems,
and find a better way to live our story together.

Chapter 6: Odd Love

The madness of love is the greatest of heaven's blessings.
Plato, Phaedrus (370 BC)

Quirky Love

Love is frequently confusing,
unpredictable and bizarre,

A strange kaleidoscope
of words, actions and feelings,
that surprise, confuse and contradict,
often bringing lovers to our knees.

Love may childishly jump up and down,
sputter, whistle and click,
whirl and swirl,
or roll on the floor laughing.

It may adore us, then turn its back,
or build glorious masterpieces of tribute,
and throw stinking filth on them.

Love can be kind and heartless,
luscious and filling
but leave a sour stomach,
lovesick, then cynical, then hopeful again.

Love sends passionate notes
and forgets every word,
or criticizes the grammar of ardent declarations,
and smugly loses the meaning.

What clowns we become
when we play at being lovers--
blustering, blind, incredibly stupid,
repeating our limited repertoires.

None of us are immune to love's impossible madness.

Funny Love

Love makes every one of us into chumps,
again and again,
so we might as well laugh
instead of cry and stress,
it's much more restoring.

So let us chuckle at the dances we do together;
the control struggle--
push-pull,
the intimacy chase--
come closer-run away,
the blame dance--
nyah-nyah.

And laugh at the impossible dreams we savor--
that I deserve the love of my dreams,
not this fool!

We lovers can be wildly demanding,
fluttering about,
bumping into each other,
or sulking because we didn't get our way.

Love is a silly situation comedy,
and we are no less ridiculous
than Gilda Radner and Dan Aykroyd,
mugging, fussing and tussling,

We humans have such a mix
of animal and child and intellectual inside of us,
and swap masks frequently every day,

pretending to know what we're doing
like children mimicking their parents.

Of course, we fall on our faces,
so might as well laugh
at our ridiculous messes and spectacular
failures
in the game of love.

Love Faces

Any of us not lost in our own wonderland
will be tickled to spy
the signs of love's glow on the faces
of our fellow travelers--

There's the moony face with glowing eyes,
the oogley face with the twisted mouth,
the sexy face that's hot to trot,
the pouty face like a sad puppy dog,
the heavenward-leaning goofy face,
the flirty face with twinkly eyes,
the blitzed ecstasy face like a deer in headlights,
the pleading, *please look at me* face,
the desperate, *please stay with me* face,
the peeved, *don't disrespect me* face,
the sulky, *I'm hurt* face,
the sunny, *I love you anyway* face,
and more…

Only truly kind friends
can see these faces without laughing
and calling them ridiculous, or mad,
or both,
because they remind us that love
can deprive us of all reason.

Personal Mess Love

Personal disasters can be quite embarrassing
when they result from doing
what we fully intended not to do,
anyway
(side to side head waving).

These are common events in life,
coming from our stubborn refusal
to think before acting or speaking
(wince, shrug).

Then we splatter our stupid messes
all over ourselves, and inevitably,
over those we love,
though they tried to tell us
(pointing the wagging finger).

This temporary deafness
can push loved ones away,
though it can also screen out
those whose love is only surface
(eyebrows raised, nodding head).

Those who really love us
will sit by the sidelines
through our crying and thrashing,
and wait for us to quiet down
(tilted face, pout),

And then join us on our trash heap of folly,
put their arms around us

and say, *You OK now?*
(grin).

Chapter 7: Painful Love

The practice of love offers no place of safety. We risk loss, hurt, pain. We risk being acted upon by forces outside our control.
bell hooks, *All About Love: New Visions* *(2001)*

Repentant Love

We are heavy with regret
for failing you.

We were too reactive and unthinking,
and feel utterly wretched
for the hardships and pain we caused,
or may yet cause.

We are so sorry for this error
of our judgment,
our thinking,
our skill,
our care.

We hope to speak and act
with more consideration,
to build mutual safety,
and find our way back to friendliness
and hopefully, trust.

Please find whatever forgiveness you can
manage,
while we find the courage
to face our faults
and try to become a better person.

Trauma Love

The violence of trauma crushes our spirits,
leaving us dazed and defeated.

So we may search for something beyond that
desolation,
something with substance we might embrace
to restore our faith in goodness,

Something that can provide some purpose,
to overcome this ordeal.

This urge can make us turn to
family, friends, teachers,
other helpers,
to knit together the pieces of our lives.

But often, when we find someone kind,
who listens, and holds, our truth,
our disturbed minds may doubt them,
run from them,
or attack them,
because we cannot bear
their touching our pain.

We may push away those who care,
preferring bitterness for company.

If we are fortunate, someone might
have compassion for our cynical heart
and stay,

though we may keep pushing them away
before we let their love in.

The broken among us both seek love
and mistrust it,
both search for it
and criticize it,
until something shifts inside
and we recognize that our wounded vision
mistrusts everything.

We must face our inner damage
with gentle concern
to soften our disturbed mind
and revive our faith
(bit by bit).

Eventually, we may wake up
from our misery,
to find love
is still a possibility.

Love of the Departed

The empty chair invites thinking
about the dear one who has died
and how they touched our lives.

We can cherish our memories of them,
their influences, their qualities,
and hold them in our present lives
like a nugget in our pocket.

There is nothing wrong with keeping loved ones
alive in our thoughts,
or savoring their images and expressions of
spirit,
as we do with great thinkers of the past.

We can still talk with them,
discuss questions and worries,
remember or imagine their answers,
confront them about unresolved issues,
and share our hidden feelings.

If they don't hear our words,
we are still changing our psychic framework,
by pushing through old limits.

If they do hear us,
it could change the path of their soul.

Losing a loved one makes us reckon with
the inescapable certainty of impermanence,

that we all will leave, and be left by,
everyone we care for.

We hope that all our departed loves knew
how much they meant to us.
We hope they knew the warmth
we felt in their company.

Deathless Love

When we finally move past
the organic waves of grief,
the possibility opens
for love to become deathless.

As we heal, we may see our lost beloved's
essences
as dozens of spirit fragments--
words, images, actions,
truths, knowledge,
that we still have access to--
and now we have discernment
to sort through them
with greater heart-space.

We may come to understand our beloved's
reality bits,
and sort out our negative contributions
(useless drama roles)
during our mutual story,
so we can see how it all fits together
for everyone's benefit,
and let go.

Some of these discoveries may sting
of failures, or bad judgment,
but these should diminish as our vision expands
to fully comprehend the messes we made
in our mutual passion play.

As time further calms emotions and defenses,
we can gradually release blaming
and other sadnesses of the ancestors,
to let our departed love's goodness rise,
and take a bigger part of our memories.

When that soul relationship becomes revealed,
grief will slowly give way to gratitude
for the enduring moments
that we want to treasure
from their temporary presence.

And as we celebrate our loved one's essence,
without all that junk in the way,
our love can become more and more clear,
unfettered, deathless.

We assume the walls between realms
are solid concrete--
how can that be?

Los Dias de los Muertos teach
that the dead resemble
everything in our universe--
filmy glimpses of forms
that visit and slip away.

Love's Ending

Love's traces, however deep,
are forever marked
by our human endings,
whether the sorrowful loss of death,
the painful severance of rejection,
or the quiet doom of growing indifference.

The circumstances of how love leaves us,
place the final dressings, colors and flavors
on how we remember a beloved face.

Our final moments together
leave prominent tracks on our imaginations
that can obscure reams of memories
of wonderful, profound or deeply intimate
times spent together.

An ugly fight, cutting words, suffering,
careless actions, a horrendous tragedy,
may leave a terrible impression
that pollutes years of caring and delight
with disturbing feelings.

Hurtful final words can link pain to more pain,
while kind words, or a sincere loving declaration,
can unlock and link a few precious moments
from a life of struggle
into an epic story of overcoming.

Chapter 8: Restorative Love

*Hatred and bitterness can never cure the
disease of fear; only love can do that.
Hatred paralyzes life; love releases it.
Hatred confuses life; love harmonizes it.
Hatred darkens life; love illuminates it.*
Martin Luther King Jr., *Strength to Love*
(1963)

Love's Secrets

In the whirling chaos of loving others,
there are constant stressful trials,
and sometimes those tests come
one after the other,
wearing us down,
pushing us to the edge,

And just before our strength gives in,
many of us get confused and wonder,

What have I missed?
Where did I go wrong?
This insanity cannot be love!

But love does not follow our expectations,
or interfere in the bumpiness of life,
it holds back its magic,
letting good and dull and horrid play out,
to suddenly ambush us
with overpowering sweetness,
ahhh...Ahhh,
until we submit to love's purposes again.

Over the ages we have searched for the secrets
for coping with love's disappearing acts,
but only quiet endurance
(with patience, kindness, gratitude and faith)
seems to help us
ride out the waves that smash us about,
and minimize the damage to all parties.

Love will test us constantly,
forcing us to push and stretch
our small ideas about it
into a grander palace
(including torture chambers).

We, mere humans, can never know it fully,
just continue to be loving
and expand our love minds
as far as we can bear.

Healing Love

Life's ordeals hurt our spirits
as much as anything else,
damaging our faith in people, in life,
or in ourselves.

We often have no choice
but to retreat
and hide in darkness,
but that makes it hard
for love to find us.

We must pry ourselves open
to let love hear our cries,

And bring our wound into the light
revealing the contours of its damage,
so the knotted places can relax
and breathe.

We must open to let in love's cleansing flow,
like a slow, gentle river,
so it washes away dirt and clotted blood,
until the wound is clean.

Or, let love work like a mouse
chewing holes, one by one,
in the straightjacket of our errors,
slowly freeing us so we barely notice
as those heavy bindings fall off.

We can release
our burdens to love,
and let its healing support us
in rediscovering our story--
to see, with tender eyes,
our whole mess of pain and promise,
and begin again.

Tough Love

Taking weakens the character,
creating adult-sized children
with petty hearts and giant appetites,
who think nothing of using others
or enslaving them to their needs.

To prevent spoiled children from
growing into adult monsters
every day they must be challenged
to limit their voracious hungers
and to hear others' voices.

The art of tough love means
saying "no" a thousand times,
challenging someone's selfish grabbing,

Guiding them to compassion for others,
so they can listen, be respectful,
and practice healthy responding
to interactions of all colors and stripes.

Tough love strives for a world in balance,
that works for happier individuals
through partnerships that nourish all.

Honest Love

Sees ignorance harming those we care for,
and dares speak what they fear to know.

Honest love is a deeper love of essence
that conveys a wish for the possible,
to be one's fullest and best self
with no need to hide.

But honest love does not feel loving
when given or received--
it torments the truth teller with nightmares of loss
and countless questions of benefit,

Truthful love can be shocking to receive,
bringing searing shame or outrage
to have the buried laid out and named.

Because when the denied truth is revealed
it risks disrupting our comfort--
loved ones may flee,
or hate us for pointing it out.

Often, we refuse to listen when love disagrees,
challenging our illusions and pride,

We may attack the messenger
to avoid confronting the self-serving illusions
that keep us from seeing better choices,
in the forever human struggle
with facing our shadows.

Honest love asks us to commit to loving
with fierce intentions to learn from wrongs,
fierce courage to push beyond defenses,
and fierce faith in working out truths together,

Instead of ignorantly going on,
pretending that everything is just fine.

Strong Love

When love holds truth in its hands
despite the stormy ugliness it reveals,
love develops its muscles.

When love shields its vision
to hide from the unpleasant imperfect,
it grows flabby and weak.

Strong love can bear arguments,
betrayal, despair, neglect,
being pushed away,
or eons of annoying dullness,
yet it continues to be loving,
working to restore friendliness
through kind responses
again and again.

It has faith that love's moments of treasure
are worth the price of dealing with
mountains of idiocy, pain and neglect.

Strong love holds on
no matter what comes into view
then digs deep into the rubble of wasted
memories
for the glowing embers needed
to revive its fires.

Strong love trusts in the ultimate goodness
of those we hold dear,

lets go of what does not matter,
and stays in the room.

Graceful Love

Wants to support each person it regards,
no matter what they've done,
no matter how ignorant or hateful they may be,
it claims the higher ground
and responds with loving energy,
even when it doesn't make sense.

Graceful love wants to help everyone
find their way through life's mazes
and fulfill their best wishes,
so they can shine.

Graceful love recognizes the contours and flows
of interactions,
sees their workings with a positive frame,
cherishes their hidden beauty and power,
and sends support, respect and gratitude
into the process.

Graceful love does this work lightly,
ever aware that pushing too hard
makes any gift of love
difficult to receive.

Space Love

It is easy to fall in love with space
because of its amazing powers
to protect and set boundaries,
to move and change us,
to help us grow and flower,

But infatuation with those powers
may lead us to overuse space
and become imbalanced
between making space for me,
and making space for we.

We might adore space so much,
we kill a relationship with too much distance,
starving it of intimacy juice.

Remember to use space
as an instrument of love,
to give us time
to recharge,
to breathe and unfold,
to sort out confusion,
to heal our hearts and minds,
to wake us up to see our path.

We must also create loving space for
relationships
so our union gets the energy it needs

to be nourished, to grow,
to find balance,
to deal with challenges,
and to heal from the countless bruises
that come with life together.

In all our interconnected relations,
the power of space
must be shared with a generous heart
so that everyone has a chance to flourish
as individuals and in relationships.

Love Energy

I. Love Energy's Work

Love is an energy form,
a deep resonance
that links and sustains everyone
and everything.

Love energy nourishes us
with the living atmosphere that we breathe,
while it energizes protective dynamics
within our interconnected emotional presence.

We feed one another many energy frequencies,
a hundred times a minute,
gradually shaping our interpersonal climate
for good or ill.

Love is the nurturing, supportive force
that provides our base connection,
and is the glue that holds us together
as it nourishes our caring bonds
and builds acceptance within our mutual
community.

II. Finding Love Energy

In every communication between beloveds,
some caring can be found,
even when other motives dominate.

If we can ignore the distractions--
the drama,

the intellectual frills,
the insecure, controlling and defensive moves,
we might discover love's energy working
quietly, under the surface.

We must look for love wherever we go,
become aware of it radiating from our core,
feel the warm flow connecting us,
explore its presence in situations,
watch for its affectionate glances and touches.

We who believe in love
must contribute to love's work
in order for love to survive in our terrible times.

III. Love Energy Magic

As we dig love energy up
and wash the muck from its gleaming face,
we gladden it
and empower its magic.

We can develop our love vision
and become love energy magicians,
planting and growing love around us,
and spinning love's healing energy
so others can be moved by love.

Love magicians can channel love energy
with a word,
a touch,
a look.

Love energy is the great healer of the world,
it frees us from fear
and helps us grow more compassionate,
while deepening our bonds with all life.

Chapter 9: Love Work

Have compassion for everyone you meet,
even if they don't want it. What seems
conceit, bad manners, or cynicism is always
a sign of things no ears have heard, no eyes
have seen. You do not know what wars are
going on down there where the spirit meets
the bone.
"Compassion" by Miller Williams,
from *The Ways We Touch*: *Poems* (1997)

Balancing Love

Most of us pursue our own desires
with little regard for others,
forgetting that one-sided relationships
are not sustainable,
and eventually crash.

Look at the mess of human relations
in our age, on every level,
there is so much division and abuse
due to our self-serving mentalities.

I. Balancing Micro Relationships

So often, we neglect our beloveds,
do not listen,
and take too much,
ignoring the grief we leave behind.

When selfishness is reflexive, an unchanging
pattern,
it withers the giver and makes the taker
top-heavy and irresponsible.

When anyone is regularly deprived
in sacrificing for our benefit,
they gradually sicken,
whatever the façade may say.

II. Balancing Macro Relationships

In our world community, the dominance of greed
is eating everything pure and beautiful

and leaving the rest to waste,
poverty, injustice and war.

When there is no balance,
justice withers to a mean skeleton,
with no concern or civility.

Our mercenary rulers do not realize
that we cannot stay healthy
when any group is disempowered or abused
within our fields of influence
and that the living world thrives best
in adaptive equity.

III. Balancing Work

In our relations, large and small,
the work of balancing is tremendous—

To challenge our self-serving thinking
to not justify disrespect and thievery,

To hear and value the needs of others
while respecting ourselves,

To equalize workload, stress load,
support, and power to do as we like,
in our intimate circles
and greater communities.

Few of us know balanced love,
so we must seek it,
negotiate it,
push for it,

and create it
with every moment
in order to empower harmony
out of our devastation.

Parent Love

Is the backbone of civil society,
holding the human race up
with care and guidance,

Parent love cares for young ones
despite nonstop demands,
and too many common heartbreaks
that parents must bear.

Every intentional parent wants to love their
children,
and most who failed or withered
began in love,
but could not bear the hardships.

Someone should remind
defeated mothers and fathers
that it's never too late--
that the Parent-Child bond
can be healed
through the heart's great capacity
to reach out lovingly.

Parent love holds out cradling arms
for all the world's babies,
caressing and nurturing our vulnerable ones,
soothing their hurts and confusion,

Aching with tenderness for them,
that they may survive
and find their way.

Mother Love

Is a fundamental benevolent power
that emanates a nurturing flow
from deep within Earth,
that generates life forms
and supports their growth into fullness.

Mother love does its best to manage
the complex and endless work of caretaking,
guiding young spirits
and anxiously watching them stumble
through the dangerous mazes of development,
and agonizing when unable to intervene.

The protective strength of mothers is legendary--
often stronger than an elephant
while heroically triumphing over monsters
who threaten their babies.

Millions of mothers are tirelessly generous and
kind--
working long hours caring for others,
comforting the discouraged and hurt,
feeding crowds with a smile
even when weary and overtaxed,
so their motherly hearts may suffer sometimes
from too much denying of self-needs.

Mothers may also become drained
by these constant exertions and complex
judgments,

but they are necessary to help fledglings survive
in our predatory world.

Mothers' work may also be suppressed
by hatred of female strength
that can leave them brutalized and broken,
sometimes so wounded,
they abandon their young.

Mother love may also be limited by fear,
when their obsessing on harms
can hold children back
or seek to control their flight.

Although they frequently fail,
most mothers work hard to help their children
survive,
and those who protect too much,
or push too hard
join legions of fools of human error
and often pay a heavy price.

Still, mother love endures
caring for the Earth's babies,
helping them take flight,
and grieving for them when they are gone.

This heavenly treasure,
that can always be tapped into
by anyone called to be a mother.

Mother love supports the flames of love among
us,

and keeps us vitally linked to each other
and to the living earth.

Father Love

May be invisible,
taken for granted--
the steady work,
the strong presence,
the helping hand.

Father love can be limited by masculine rules
against nurturing and softness,
so dads may be reduced to family disciplinarian,
showing the right way,
something all children need
but are seldom grateful to experience.

Fortunate fathers can correct children
with strategic words and solutions,
teach them instead of control them,
leaving a legacy of knowledge
that discipline can be paired with love
instead of violence.

Father love is less imprinted than mothering--
many men see few examples to follow
and remain uneasy
because their fathers were not available
to show how to connect to children
or comfort childish feelings,

Many fathers have trouble finding words,
and join their children

through rough and tumble play
to convey affection and support,

Or they may say little,
filling the void with bravado,
electronics or alcohol.

When fathers do speak,
their words are powerful--
written on our hearts,
whether inspiring or hurtful,
remaining with us for lifetimes.

Father love carries an ancient burden
of punishment and wounding,
but as that painful legacy is revealed,
they are working through the rocky middle
of the change process,
towards healing.

Fathers do the best that they can
and mourn their failings to be the father they
want to be.
They stress about the sicknesses of the world
and the troubles they will bring to their families.

Please remember, fathers are here for love--
they try to be there for us
through our unpleasant messes.
and most of them stay for love's purposes,
despite heavy costs.

We can support fathers in their loving work
by telling stories of good fathering,
and by noticing, remembering and celebrating
the millions of good fathers in this world.

Brother & Sister Love

Is a deep and enduring connection,
mixed with so many other feelings--
trust, care, protectiveness, loyalty,
jealousy, rivalry, hurt, worry,
and fury.

Many siblings are solid allies
through lifetimes of struggles,
while others neglect family bonds
or blame one another for every little thing.

The fortunate among us have
a devoted sibling to turn to,
for help, sympathy,
to laugh or cry with,
or calm us down.

Brothers and sisters want to know our news,
to share our joys, accomplishments and hopes,
but they will also tell us
if they don't like our choices,
or think they know better.

Siblings love to tell stories of each other's
failings,
entertaining others with each episode
of the family soap opera
(might as well laugh).

Sisters and brothers may have to struggle
to find loving responses to each other's

challenges,
disasters, losses, changes,
mistakes and acts of inconsideration,

While simple misunderstandings can take years,
even decades, to resolve
before siblings take down grudging walls.

But love between sisters and brothers
can erase old wounds in an instant
when a sibling cries for help
and suddenly, support and caring revive,
flowing everywhere,
like a river freed from a dam.

Brother and sister love is always there
behind the turmoil,
a transcending bond
that teaches us constantly
how much we need each other.

No matter what path we take,
or what life hands us,
sisters and brothers
are never alone.

Loving Teens

Half childish confusion
burdened with doubts, wounds,
and untamed vision.

Half adult standing tall,
fighting for respect,
unwilling to take the easy lies.

Contradictory, uneasy, insecure,
but underneath drama-seeking-belligerence,
they ask only for recognition and acceptance
so they can seek their unique purpose.

Still, so many of us can't hear them or see them,
and this keeps them hurt and angry
and choosing recklessness
to cope with our indifference.

It would be so easy to listen--
to honor them,
to let them be who they need to be--

So they can find that something beautiful
inside
to bring to the world.

Grandparent Love

Grandparents listen to a child's woes,
to try to understand,
to help them feel better,
giving some guiding wisdom
and a sheltering hug.

Grandparents can be playful,
coming to a child's point of view
wanting to see their fort,
their heroes, their villains,
and all the other characters
and meanings in their lives,
as if they matter.

They know that parenting is overwhelming
and prone to many mistakes,
so they want to fill in,
to help their own child-parent
find their ultimate healing.

Aging Love

Is gentle, kind, ethereal,
sometimes too delicate
to draw our attention,
despite its wisdom,
great patience and humor.

As we trudge through the petty wars
and social dramas of life,
loving becomes wiser--
better able to see beyond expectations,
hurts, grudges, stupidity,
and social prejudices.

Life is a punishing teacher,
but we who are able to endure
and keep our hearts open
develop a penetrating vision.

Even great horrors can be softened,
to be seen as one of many sad episodes
in humanity's journey.

After many years of enduring life's cruelties,
we can feel gratitude
for every ray of light,
and discover amusement
in every wrinkle and sigh.

Self-Love

Is not savoring our greatness,
spelling out accomplishments,
or constantly indulging desires.

It's not bolstering our ego by criticizing others
or holding ourselves superior.

Self-lovers need no outer validation
with trinkets or praise or comparisons,
we persevere when confronted with doubt.

Lovers of self do not fake perfection,
we accept the misjudgments of living
as necessary teachers
instead of faults
to hide from in shame.

Being a friend to ourselves in times of stress,
helps restore inner serenity,
making us less prone to the reactive stupidity
that sabotages our relationships
and our lives.

Self-love means being the friend and ally
we've always wanted--
noting and valuing our better efforts,
and always finding compassion for our
blundering child-self.

Sweet, wholehearted love of self
can help us find enough courage

to love others through thick and thin,
and to tolerate the inevitable hurts
and random ordeals
that come with opening to the universe.

Friend Love

I. Friend Flavors

There are a thousand varieties of friends
joining in infinite ways and intensities,

From simply filling time and functions,
to being there through tragedies,
sharing dreams and secrets,
and profoundly honoring each other.

Friendships are less defined and more complex
than other relationships,
with needs, projections, other people,
conflicts and questions about choices or
perspectives,
coloring and mucking up the picture,
often making them unpredictable or messy.

Friends' roles with each other are more fluid,
lacking the structure of marriage,
living space or duties,
we may shift from ally to opponent,
from teacher to needy one.

When tragedy occurs, someone we barely know
can become our deepest confidant,
bringing out strengths and virtues,
while a trusted friend can break our spirits
for a minor misunderstanding.

Friends can lie, cheat, steal
and blame us for the offense--
perhaps these do not deserve the label,
but until a moment ago
they were good and kind.

II. Friend Soup

When we join with friends,
we become another creature,
mixing energies,
driven by each other's urgings,
for fun, exploration, conversation,
creativity, solace, anger or depravity.

How we blend is a mystery of alchemy,
for even the best of minds can make a bitter
stew,
while the careless may create delight or heroic
action.

Wounded friends may make a hurtful mess
or they may work kindness into their give and
take,
to make a sweeter soup.

The day to day energy between friends
also shifts in regular cycles and in times of
trouble,
from hot to warm or cold,
affectionate to dull or harsh,
stressful to stimulating or relaxing.

III. Friend Benefits

The love of friends can be a cascade of
miracles,
enhancing our lives through thick and thin,
but how many of us can pull it off?

The work of loving friends is so challenging--
to tolerate foolishness and insensitivity,
to talk through the urge to turn away,
to find common ground,
to forgive despite the risks.

Some friendships may leave us with a bitter
lesson,
but we must keep reaching out,

Because friends are the ultimate happiness,
whether always there, or for some nugget of
time,
they bring the support, meaning and sweetness
needed for a beautiful life.

Partner Love

Loving a partner can be the ultimate
comfort and bliss,
fire and war--

The comfort of home and protection,
mixed with occasional wars of heart and spirit,
the bliss of intimacy,
mixed with the fire of anger.

Partner love can be the relationship of our
dreams
or our nightmares,
or it can be worn out by the constant friction
of worries, frustrations and problems.

If well-matched and lucky with the elements,
our troubles may be minor,
but most couples have serious work to do,
to find our way to ten thousand awkward
compromises
and to forge an equality
that nurtures and nourishes our love.

In the partnership cauldron of psyche and
temperament and luck,
every day spent together sweetly,
and every hurt that is reconciled,

is a victory for love,
proving to the whole human race
that harmony between beloveds
can be realized.

If the union becomes broken,
partner love does not end,
our work must continue, internally and together,
to find respectful responses,
to honor both of us as worthy,
and to understand our partnership's legacy.

Loving an Ex-Partner

After the hopeful illusions have
long been buried,
and the corpse of a relationship
has become dried bones,
many ex-partners become friends.

These can be powerful friendships
born through reflection, burning conversations,
painfully wrought forgiveness,
and a morsel of love.

Failure can make us kinder, stronger and wiser,
better able to see our part
and let go of the junk.

We may be drawn
to the special flavor of that past relationship,
or just want to talk again,
to laugh at our foolishness,
to revel in our common understandings,
and to bask in the light of their sweet smile.

This other side of relationship can become
a sweet, enduring friendship
with reasonable expectations, that knows
the idiocy of all grudges,
the folly of power struggles,
and the preciousness of forgiveness.

Loving Our Neighbor

Does not interest us much these days--
neighborliness is less important, less useful,
passé'.

Our common interest in safety and peace,
no longer matters
compared to our little preferences.

Now we criticize and spy,
complain about noise and animals,
and worry about property values.

Don't block my driveway!

Few of us know our neighbor's names--
we are strangers,
unaware of trouble or tragedy
happening so close.

We could revive neighborly values,
by treating our neighbors like friends and family,
striving to be generous and kind over business,
so that we create cycles of benevolence
that can enrich the lives of those in our
neighborhood.

We could smile and wave at our neighbors,
and keep an eye on children, teens, elders,
pets and houses,
watching for trouble and mishaps.

We could even help neighbors--
bring over food and medicine,
help each other with yard and garden,
run errands, and visit
to check on each other's well-being.

Any of us can join in
to help our neighborhood enclave discover its
heart,
and thrive.

Edge Love

No love is safe,
but edge people are very risky bets
for loving, such as--

Creative geniuses,
artists and musicians,
writers and philosophers,
social activists, loners…

Anyone who sees through social pretenses,
who doesn't conform to the rules
and challenges the status quo,
may challenge our status quo too.

Most of us seek safety in boxes
to cope with life's chaos and brutality,
but edge lovers cannot bear boxes,
they have to break out
or tear them down,
sometimes disregarding the consequences
and breaking our hearts.

The ideals they are serving,
whether right or wrong, heroic or primitive,
can blind them to our feelings,
so they'll sacrifice our needs
during their next box-breaking frenzy.

Loving people on the edge
can still be an exquisite adventure
full of romantic thrills, discovery and profound
teachings,
if we meet them with strength,
demand respect,
and enjoy the moments of brilliance
created when we are together.

Love Under Oppression

When we awaken to our oppression,
the presence of feet on our neck,

We often feel a driving purpose surging,
a fire to *do something*,
to push for fairness,
speak truth to leaders,
and join movements for change.

But to do anything during these cruel times
when we are so lost
and everything is being eaten,
we must take care to not be eaten ourselves.

First, we must find some balance
between working against outrages
and retreating to restore our strength.

Second, we need to see the world's grasping
ways,
guard against them,
and yet transcend them,
overcoming them in our own dealings,
so we can empower root change.

Third, we must reach for the big picture,
a greater vision of oppression through history,
so we can discover our common heart-needs
and common sicknesses.

Fourth, we must join with others
fighting the same fight,
overcoming our differences
to know we are not alone,
to help each other with burnout,
to celebrate our successes (however small),
and to recharge our collective light.

Together with those who fight by our side
we form an incredible kinship
in our passion for a righteous cause.

Finally, we must feed our souls,
by stealing whatever moments we can
to go for joy,
by savoring life's beauty,
and finding wisdom in our difficulties
so we can let go of fear.

We need many kinds of support
when we work against oppression,
because the work is endless
and the truth can tear us apart.

Chapter 10. Love Arts

True genius without heart is a thing of nought - for not great understanding alone, not intelligence alone, nor both together, make genius.
Love! Love! Love! that is the soul of genius.
Nikolaus Joseph von Jacquin, entry in Mozart's souvenir album (1787)

Love of Words

Words connect mind to mind, heart to heart,
and spirit to spirit.

Words move us in infinite ways--
caressing, protecting, teaching,
venerating, desecrating,
belittling, battering, consoling,
dominating, dividing,
warding off, placating,
gently prying open,
pleading, cajoling,
inciting, exciting, teasing, flirting,
cherishing, understanding,
and bringing us together.

The impact of words can be visceral, like
touching,
though their traces can last much longer
and mark us more deeply than violence.

These bits of meaning reach across space
and cultural boundaries,
echoing over time, some, many lifetimes,
and can have astonishing power
to heal or harm
our troubled and divided peoples.

Some fall in love with words themselves,
becoming fascinated with their meaning layers
when arranged this way or that.

They may feel called to become word artists,
to arrange thought fragments in various ways,
to paint evocative worlds of mystery and
meaning,
or stir troubles into the fire.

Kind intentions shape words into instruments of
peace,
while the wisdom of history
shapes words into instruments of justice.

Beautiful, thoughtful, caring words
can work to unravel humanity's madnesses,
and free us from the limitations
which torment and imprison us,
as they help us share, understand, and savor
our wild, challenging journey together.

Book Love

Many books are lightweight and unchallenging,
bringing a little diversion,
a few thrills or some laughs,
if we are lucky...

While other books go deep,
delving into the unknown--
the many layers of suffering,
the faces of evil,
the tortures of loneliness,
the pain of abuse,
the absurdity of our human predicament.

Some volumes suck us in without warning,
breaking our hearts with agonies
or thrilling our mind with possibilities.

Books can raise forgotten communities back into
aliveness,
and bring breath to someone long dead,
so they can whisper their secrets to us.

Book authors may lurk inside the play of words,
revealing desires, biases and wisdom,
or engaging and probing their readers.

Some books are tossed away quickly,
while others require a commitment,
taking weeks to study and absorb,
or years.

Books may become lifelong friends and
mentors,
helping us through difficulties,
teaching us how to find meaning
in times of chaos or despair.

We spend so much time with the books we
cherish,
with the hearts and minds within them,
that they may mark our lives as deeply
as any person we love.

Poet Love

Is soft, sweet and caressing,
or deep, revealing and passionate,
or intense and provoking,
or analytical and obtuse,
or foolish and silly,
depending on the poet
or the subjects involved.

Poets labor away their days
to create word gifts for us,

Working to uncover
what needs expression,
constantly searching for ways to shape ideas,
phenomena, feelings, energy,
sacrificing sleep or interrupting occasions
to write down precious fragments of meaning.

Poets suffer for what their vision
opens them to,
and often cannot tolerate stupefying
time-wasting
(unless resting their muses).

Poets serve the voices that visit them,
adoring the worlds they offer,
while fearing their abandonment
to voiceless days
or years.

Music Love

Music lifts our souls with its healing breezes,
that lighten our daily grind.

It wakes up the senses,
inspiring us to move, to activate, to dance.

Music's sweetness can help the wooden to
weep
and console them in their weeping,
while its loving power comforts and soothes,
comforting those in crisis,
giving hope to the broken,
uniting communities and cultures.

But music's power is not limited
to those with good intentions--
it has fueled ages of drug binges, abuse and
violence,
so its influence must be used with care.

Still, music works mainly for love--
its great strength moves us,
stimulates creativity,
transforms confusion into clarity
and inspires us to open up our thinking
to consider other views.

Millions have given their lives
to create these arrangements of sound,
generously working year upon year,

to soothe and inspire us,
with little financial reward (for most).

Yet, it is worth it--
to participate in the delivery of magic
and to feel music's blessings
as they pass through.

Music's love can inspire us to make bad times
into turning points,
pushing us outside of our mindsets,
to move our energy and let go,
so we can play with the pieces of whatever is
happening,
change our direction,
and journey on.

Lover's Menu

1. Dating Special

Tossed baby green salad with shredded carrots.
Several tapas (dishes from many cultures)
for tasting and comparing.
Italian cream cake with wild berries
(if you still have an appetite).

2. New Lovers' Special

An extravagant antipasto platter with a mélange
of olives, marinated veggies,
smoked and aged cheeses.
Grilled purple asparagus.
Several luscious ravioli dishes to share.
Café mocha with almond biscotti.

3. Burning Lovers' Special

Grilled figs stuffed with goat cheese and basil.
A large platter of savory grilled proteins
and veggie chunks on skewers.
A bowl of whole, ripe pears
served with a basket of hot washcloths.

4. Committed Lovers' Special

Raw vegetable plate with low-calorie dip.
Broiled fillet served with garlicky greens.
Sweet wine and bittersweet chocolate,
plus a fortune cookie.

5. Bitter Lovers' Special

Pickled fruit appetizer plate.
Two servings of well-cooked stew
in a sauce with notes of acidity and heat.
served with dry toast.
Tequila Sunrises.

6. Reconciling Lovers' Special

Crab bisque for two.
Potato hash with yesterday's meat and cream
gravy.
Grilled sweet and spicy peppers.
Lemon sorbet with a butter cookie.

7. Old Lovers' Special

Crusty hot peasant bread with soft Irish butter.
A large, gorgeous green salad to share
full of crunchy, sour and savory-sweet delights,
plus a few chewy bits,
with creamy and spicy dressings on the side.
Cherries Jubilee to finish.

Love's Taste

The taste of love is sweet and delicate--
smooth on the tongue,
melting slowly,
revealing complex fruity flavors
and a hint of bitter spices
beneath the taste of honey.

The first bites release buttery sweet juices
that caress and pleasure our mouth,
then later, we come to the tough, thick-skinned
core,
which can only be softened by chewing
patiently,
and swallowing a few remaining chunks.

Love can be tough as leather,
but never sickens if we take it in
small bites.

Love's Smell

Love smells like animals
healthy, furry bodies
carrying the smell of earth
and damp woods.

Love's smell turns bad
when neglected.
The smell of decay arises
along with sharp scents of sourness,
making our noses twinge.

Love's Feel

Love feels warm, soft and round
like a sleeping kitten,
it undulates to our touch
as we stroke its silky fur,
though the playful paw
may strike out to wound
the hand it loves.

When love is used for ill,
it will become a cold, hard cadaver,
springing to life if bumped,
with teeth and claws tearing at you until
you are wounded,
and show your tender heart again.

Love's Hands

Reach out--

Touch*

Comfort,

(Hold)

Caress.

Ache

Burn with need!!!

Express!

<u>Draw the line</u>

--Push away--

Plead?

Beckon...

Chapter 11: Love Manifestations

Love all of God's creation, the whole and every grain of sand of it. Love every leaf, every ray of God's light. Love the animals, love the plants, love everything. If you love everything, you will perceive the divine mystery in things. Once you perceive it, you will begin to comprehend it better every day. And you will come at last to love the whole world with an all-embracing love.
Fyodor Dostoevsky (Father Zossima speaking), *The Brothers Karamazov*, (1879)

Love of Earth

Is wonder
at Earth's growing green richness--
lush savannas, sheltering forests and
mountains,
and generous waters flowing and serenely
waiting.

Her lavish offerings nurture our senses
with so much magnificence,
while supporting every life form in turn.

Love of Earth is fascination and respect
for her countless creatures--
grand carnivores, omnivores and herbivores,
animals with flashing speed, deep social bonds,
or ingenious survival tricks,
the amazing wonders of sea creatures,
the incredible inventiveness of insects,
and the microscopic life that infuses all
in our cycles of health and disease.

Love of Earth means gratitude and awe
for Earth's dynamic powers,
the vital energy that lives under our feet,
and the awesome power of the waters,
winds, flames, and earth masses around us.

It means perceiving Earth's life signs,
witnessing her spirit inhaling, exhaling,
groaning and laughing

as the human race busily scrapes
and stomps on her body.

Love of Earth means sensing her infinite
blessings
to all her children
with each breath and heartbeat.

Wilderness Love

The power of wild lands to enchant us
far transcends their postcard beauty,
or even the magical music of water's fall
and sounds of birds, insects and frogs.

Wild nature's power to heal and restore
is a mystery that can only be known
through time and silence,
putting aside our tamed minds to feel
nature's pulsing.

Being alone and quiet is the only way
to compel the forests, fields and desert lands
to reveal their beating hearts.

Time in silence opens us to nature's green fire,
allowing it to burn through our crusted senses
and brand us with a scar
whose tenderness we savor.

That wound forever connects us
to nature's living flesh,
making us ache when we learn about abuses
of forests, fields, creatures, water bodies,
whenever earth is ripped open or poisoned,
another sacrifice to brutish greed.

Wilderness lovers obsess about these losses
feeling every episode of nature's agony
inside,

And would give anything
to stop these offenses
and save our wild treasures.

Animal Love

There is a primal love connection
between people and animals,
whether household pets, farm or wild.
Animal love is a deep energetic cord
that gives and takes both ways,
though we often don't notice it.

I. Pet Love

With animal pets,
the love cord speaks of need and protection,
deep mutual alliances
of shelter and sustenance.

Pets may serve as guardians of our homes,
holding newcomers at bay,
testing their intentions,
or welcoming visitors who please.

Many pets and their people struggle
to get their way with each other,
a frequent interspecies control drama
that many humans cannot master
(or don't try).

The presence of animals in our homes
grounds and nurtures us,
stirs our energies, stretches us,
and reminds us of our animal instincts.

II. Farm Animal Love

With farm animals,
the cord speaks of sustenance.
We feed them,
and whether we eat them or not
our world has been shaped
around their flesh.

Cows, chickens, pigs, and other "stock"
have become slaves to human profit-minds,
helpless against the conditions of their
existence.

When we give them gentle care and space
they will greet us, listen to us
and fuss about goings-on
as they share life on our farms.

If we neglect, confine or torment farm animals,
their diseases and sadness
will infect and demean us.

III. Wild Animal Love

With wild animals,
the connection speaks of survival--
Which of us belongs here?
Are you a threat?
Which of us is food?

We may study their animal ways,
display or make animal art,

trying to capture their essence
or to emulate their earthy strengths.

Sometimes we are blessed to encounter wild
ones
and safely make contact in their territory
to see beyond fear
and find mutual respect between our wild souls.

IV. Loving Animals

Humans are also animals--
we pursue our appetites,
protect our vulnerability,
and move around our territories
looking for resources to stay alive...
so why don't we consider their plight?

Every day, animals offer us deep lessons
in how to live in the world,
teaching us their earth medicine
and touching us with their hidden wizardry.

Even if we never interact with animals,
we still share the circle of life,
where animals profoundly enrich our lives
with their power, beauty and wisdom.

Cat Love

Is self-contained,
not offering itself to us
without absolute trust
and anticipation of pleasure.

If we learn their language and ways,
we may become valued as an ally,
and occasionally spy signs
of adoration.

We who meet their criteria
may be rewarded with affection--
a soft cooing call,
the touch of a gentle paw,
or sweetly nestling down their fuzzy round
forms,
as they nuzzle into leg hollows, shoulders,
bellies,
and sweetly purr their appreciation.

Dog Love

Dogs are such loving souls
and welcoming friends,
full of gratitude
for our ordinary company.

If you are lonely,
depressed, confused,
or broken-hearted,
a dog's love can heal you.

And, if you love them
they will remind you of care,
that is their nature.

Our canine friends sacrifice profoundly
for their caretakers,
helping us for good or ill,
giving such loving service,
constantly forgiving our carelessness
or enduring our abuse.

Dogs are shaped to the bone for our needs,
our connection habits,
our playfulness and sports,
our lovingness or meanness,
our routines and our wealth--
protecting our homes and our lives,
serving our blood sports
and playing a part in so many human
obsessions.

Dogs could be our sin-eating angels,
because they take into their beings
what we can't face
with their loving acceptance,
and so, heal our calloused hearts.

Tree Love

Trees are the great silent lovers of our world,
adoring sky and sun,
while gently caressing Earth
and nurturing her waters.

Their strength, generosity and grace inspire us
as they reach out and up to the heavens
and dive into the earth,
generously working for love's purposes.

Trees provide shelter for hundreds of creatures
under their arms,
protecting communities of birds, animals,
insects and other plant life,
and supporting other trees through root
networks.

These many-armed beings
clean and enrich our air,
protect and fertilize our lands,
call in the clouds to bring rain,
and leave their gorgeous flesh
to be used for shelter, heat and art.

Trees ask little and do so much
to heal our troubled planet,
but humanity is not so generous in return--
we cut and shred trees,
poison their soil and water,

and bulldoze their sweet communities
for our petty pleasures.

Trees feel these attacks in their collective soul--
whole forests sicken
and mourn for their companions,
so the love of trees diminishes,
losing their power to protect Earth and her
creatures.

Trees also feel our support
when we nurture or protect them,
and bless with quiet peace
those of us who call them family.

Gardeners' Love

Gardeners adore the smell and feel of dirt--
moist, rich, soft soil is heaven to us.

We can sense living energy
within that soft clump of earth
and its billions of pulsing organisms.

We who love gardens
savor visions of luminescent green threads
undulating up from below earth's covers
to unfold into generous forms
that gratify and nourish.

Gardeners are loving gods
managing water and energy,
life and death,
and inspiring renewal

As we guide, protect, support and harvest
our little universes
season after season.

Water Love

It may be the water inside us
that constantly seeks water out there,

That gazes at water's glistening forms
as it rises and falls,
and listens to its healing melodies,
savoring these blessings inside,
perhaps feeling a quiet release,
remembering our gentle womb-cradle.

The pulsing rivers inside us might sense
the life force flowing in waterways,
and follow their patterns
as they divide and shape earth,
settling into lakes and oceans
that birth and churn with life.

Water's angelic drops sink deep into
the flesh of earth
infusing millions of capillaries with juices,
to revive the seeds of life nestled within
and nourish those sprouts into growth
to fill our world with chattering.

When we touch water,
our skin cells tingle and open to its caressing
as it washes away scum and grit,
and freshens us for living.

When we drink water, it awakens our bodies,
sweetly filling our soft tissues

while coursing through thousands of channels within,
muscles, organs, bones, nerves...

Water is generous in her loving work
and despite all we do to steal her powers and pollute her,
she continues her healing work
with the shreds of her power.

Sky Love

Draws our attention upward
to the powerful peace of space
while its supportive power soaks into us,
filling our cells with pure living flow.

Sky's light energy crowns us
and embraces us
whenever we go outside.

By day its glowing blueness
softens and inspires our minds,
reflecting the sun's blinding fire
to keep us warm.

Sky love may change constantly
when decorated with clouds
expressing countless works of art--
quaking dark masses,
billowing waves of color,
or slender shimmers,
while birds fly in elegant patterns.

By night the sky
is a hushed and peaceful temple,
decorated with sparkling gems,

While the sweet glowing moon
adores us full on,
and then hides its face
like any other lover.

Love of Place

What gives a place such magic
that it haunts our dreams,
pushes aside our logic,
and pulls us back
seeking *something* there?

Some places are unforgettable,
their sounds and images echo inside.

It's a different location for each of us--
a loud and busy city,
a waterfront refuge,
a cozy small town,
a majestic forest or mountain.

It could be the physical nature of place
that moves us--
high settings with gorgeous views,
green halls of tree branches,
glistening grasslands,
deserts with vast skies,
currents of healing waters,

Carefully crafted old buildings,
a beloved town square,
a familiar neighborhood caring for families,
or a regular booth in the corner
where friends share their lives.

It could be the spirit of a place--
the kindness of plain country folk,

its cherished traditions, humble honesty,
spirited art scene, celebrated music,

Or the security of community acceptance--
warm hands and smiles greeting us,
You are welcome here.

Beloved places may remind us
of cherished parts of our lives--
identity, purpose, or peace of mind,
that we crave to return to.

Coffeehouse Love

Coffeehouses are the heart of a town,
providing shelter and emotional refuge
from the pressures of life
that too often say
not enough,
and from a world that shouts
me, me, me, and *buy, buy, buy.*

Coffeehouses provide quiet places
for reading and contemplation,
with warm beverages
and cozy places to sit,
they help us center, take measure,
and find a bit of sweet comfort.

Coffeehouses are the essence of kindly
accommodation,
with gentle spaces to meet friends
to check-in beyond our surface lives.

They give us precious solitude
when we long to calm our minds
and help us unlock the words held inside.

Many thanks to all the people
who make our coffeehouses happen,
and those who work there for so little,
to keep our community's heart beating.

Loving a Town

Every town has a character, a spirit,
that talks to and touches us,
like a giant mother animal
holding her many ant-like children.

Towns and cities are living, breathing entities
of people, systems, buildings, streets and parks
with skills, flaws, arteries, and pockets.

We can tell much about a town from its
appearance,
the patterns of wear, the care of streets and
buildings,
and its welcoming, pushy or indifferent attitude.

Cities and towns can be as mixed-up as any of
us--
with low self-esteem (doubting their value),
or anxious and worrisome (complaining and
moaning),
or vain (admiring their faces in the mirror).

It's helpful to love our town honestly,
with an outsider's appreciation
of the town's essence,
the architectural flow and curves,
the energy dynamics,
the art, the music, the culture
and spirit of its people.

But we must also study our town's downward
dynamics
because they may trample us
when we are weak or down.

If we find a town that fits and balances us
with its gifts and strengths,
it can provide a cozy nest
and open the sky for flying.

Love of Nation

We who deeply love our nation
can strive for wisdom in our pride.
We can honestly bask in the glow of our
achievements,
but still be concerned about our problems.

We have no need to be arrogant and bossy
(denying all faults),
or persecuting those who disagree.

Nation lovers can encourage each other
to work for solutions,
and use our voices to press our leaders
to support our health and social well-being,
so families and communities can grow stronger.

History shows that our nation thrives
when we unite our strengths,
when we listen and explore differences openly,
when we strive to understand each other.

If we want to be the best society,
we must balance everyone's best good skillfully,
because when people are treated right,
they give back.

We who love our nation want to contribute,
to clean our neighborhoods and schools,
to repair streets and bridges,
to protect our children,
to teach our youth respect and love of

knowledge,
and to give everyone a chance,
including those who are different or discouraged.

We can pull through
these divisive and difficult times,
if we come together to honor equality and
justice,
the ideals that have always strengthened us.

Nation lovers can learn to value and respect all
who share our stewpot (everyone),
for the flavors and perspectives,
the courage, knowledge and skills
that they contribute
to our mutual adaptability
and strength.

World Love

Somehow our crazy, battered world
keeps going, keeps working,
despite endless wars, terrible famines,
disasters and immense atrocities
that tear at the senses and reason.

It must be love
that keeps us together,

That keeps us traveling the same roads,
greeting each other, mourning disasters,
celebrating rescues and heroes,
applauding the deaths of dictators
and the triumphs of people's causes.

Anyone looking would feel awed by these
worldwide displays
of compassion and camaraderie.

Most of us treasure our world,
our striving peoples, cultures and cities,
our history of struggles and acts of great
courage.

But while we adore the world's noble side,
we must come to terms with the ugly side--
how the powerful exploit and scapegoat,
leaving behind devastated families,
communities and lands.

The meanness of our world can be so
overwhelming
that many turn in fury
on anyone who speaks of it,
or worse, questions it,

But if we accept the suffering of so many
of our brothers and sisters,
and ignore the ongoing devastation
of our sheltering Earth,
we become accomplices in world suicide.

To love the whole world,
we must break through our fearfulness,
and stop pushing the undesired truth away,
so we can shift our appetites
to not decimate anyone,
any beings, or any thing.

We can
defy this insanity
and challenge ourselves to become a kinder,
healthier world,

By cherishing the world as a whole,
its messy, beautiful complexity,
its chaotic noise music,
and magnificent endurance,

And by working together to heal our world,
to clean up our messes,
and restore our peoples, lands, waters, air,

plants and animals
to balance
for the good of all.

Chapter 12: Love Beyond Form

Love is the force that transforms and improves the Soul of the World... It is we who nourish the Soul of the World, and the world we live in will be either better or worse, depending on whether we become better or worse. And that's where the power of love comes in. Because when we love, we always strive to become better than we are.
Paulo Coelho, *The Alchemist* (1988)

Road Love

Love's journey varies tremendously
in ease and hardship
from person to person.

Some of us get good maps and smooth
pavement
while others follow scribbles on shreds of old
napkins
that lead us down treacherous, uneven roads
with hazards coming from all directions.

Most keep going,
but all of us get lost anyway,

Because when we come to forks in the road,
those major turning points,
we opt for familiar or easy,
or we don't see the better paths
because they are not on our map,

We're afraid to take a chance
on the unknown.

Real Love

Is not sweet or gentle,
not meeting someone's needs,
nor an eternal pledge--
those who live it know
these are kindergarten-pretend games.

Real love strains to behold, for five minutes,
the many-layered, ugly beauty
of the one before us,
without the usual cushioning of pretense.

Only a few weary souls can hold that
regard for more than an instant,
and they will ache with the pain
of seeing the countless tragedies
done to and by their beloved.

Real love can crush us
if our hearts are not ready,
if we do not have enough anchor to stay upright
while torrents of disregard
wash away our ground.

Really loving requires letting our whole being go
into life's flow of give and take,
giving ourselves to the grand food chain--
eating with reverence,
then letting ourselves be eaten.

When it comes to that part,
to letting go of 'me',

in that moment,
we all bare our teeth
rather than be chewed up
for someone else's nourishment.

Real love is a test between faith and fear
that leaves few of us unscarred.

Interpersonal Love

A feeling blooms within
(for whatever real or imagined reason),
becomes articulated in sounds and words,
then illustrated and orchestrated
with hundreds of information bits.

This creates a colorful energy fog
that pushes into the reality bubbles of others,
each time carrying a powerful emotional-social
matrix of influence.

As we become connected,
our positive qualities strengthen each other's
positive qualities,
while negative qualities strengthen negative
ones,
and both become energized by a complex array
of mental, emotional and social factors
within and between.

The resulting cyclone of pushes and pulls,
distils into our relationship stewpot over time,
creating internal and interpersonal patterns
that nourish or poison,
stimulate or weaken,
empower or sabotage.

How much power do we have
as individuals
to shape the outcome?
To influence the forces at work between us?
To affirm, somehow,
the good in each other,
and ourselves?

What chance do we have,
in such a jungle of pushes and pulls,
to relate honestly and live together well?
Or to create a better ending
to our story?

Systems Love

Relationships are many-legged creatures
that unite living beings
with magnetic, dynamic forces
within a chaotic, pressurized universe.

During our lives, we join many systems
and their internal and external system networks,
where we generate energy together and
intermingle frequencies
for powerful joinings, repellings or explosions
that may cause individuals, groups,
and interaction patterns
to adapt, grow, wither, or mutate.

Each of our systems has complex multileveled
flowings
that shift directions and intensities constantly
as we entities give and take constantly from
each other,
in an endless variety of dances,
creating interconnected environments that
circulate
our actions, words and energy
into some sort of exchange balance
(simultaneously in many dimensions),.

When relatively balanced, supported, and
energized,
relationship systems thrive--
spawning other systems,

nurturing beings in formation and disintegration,
challenging each other, and
exploring new dynamics of interdependent living.

Systems create and suck energy,
dominate and are dominated,
fade and disappear,
or may grow
into time-space giants.

Love of God

It's not important
whether we love an embodied God,
the Goddess,
the Great Mystery,
or the stream of consciousness moments.

What matters is that we honor something
greater than our own small, personal, temporal
ways of thinking.

It's not love to use God-talk
to support our opinions and biases,
to make ourselves comfortable,
to prop up our reputation,
or to make money.

Love of God is not saying pretty words,
not displaying images, ornaments or bumper
stickers,
and it's not blissful spiritual union,
nor even ardent prayers,
these are all using God for selfish purposes.

Those who really love God are so moved,
they put aside their self-concern and petty
prejudices,
because they are driven to open
to God's vaster purposes,
immersing themselves in serving
for love, for truth,

for grace, for kindness,
for peace.

Loving God means acting to help
whoever we can, whatever,
whenever we can,
and not getting in the way with negativity,
and condemnations.

Loving God means finding love
in everything and everyone,
and loving that bit of God manifest there
until nothing else matters.

Mother Mary's Love

Is a miraculous, compassionate power,
that softly and gently infuses our world
like the fine mist
that rises after a rainstorm.

Our Great Mother cherishes
every wounded and wretched
person or creature,
no matter how hideous
or how twisted their past.

She inspires in many forms,
from origins around the world--
Mary, Mother of God,
Maria, Guadalupe, Tonantzin,
Our Lady, Blessed Virgin,
Maryam, Miriam, Theotokos,
the Liberator, the Healer,
the Sacred Protector, the Safe Haven,
Queen of Heaven, Star of the Sea,
Mother Earth,
Honored Grandmother...

Mother Mary weeps for every one of us,
offering healing tears,
and never turns her face away.

Love of Life

Life is such a ridiculous adventure
of beauty, endeavor, deep questions,
endless doldrums, sickness, horror,
tender mercies, miraculous healings
and confusion,

But we heap suffering on each other so readily,
and the abusive jerks have us so cowed and
fearful
that it's easy to close our eyes
and hide in some version of conformity
that provides numbing distractions
to take over our days.

What a sad surrender!

There are so many paths
that bring love and joy,
if we do the work to find them
(or create them).

Why not listen for the pressures
behind life's chaos
and do something positive
instead of hiding?

Try caring for animals, or feeding wild birds,
they reward us for their sustenance
with sweet playfulness and trust.

Try rejoicing in what makes life good,
the many meaningful, friendly aspects of life
that can help us feel life's blessings,
and then join in.

So many incredible experiences are out there--
to explore, to struggle with, and to savor,
so many fascinating things to learn
about our infinitely layered world,
that will dazzle our minds

If we follow the path of awakened gratitude,
and embrace life like a lover.

Love Celebration

There is an ancient need to celebrate,
to raise our glasses to each other,
to enjoy one another's sweet company,
and smile at our good fortune
to be together.

The gifts of love, family and friendship
are so fragile and fleeting,
we must share our pleasure,
our wonder,
and our cherishing,
as often as possible.

While we live,
we must not forget to proclaim
and honor
the many miracles
of human connection.

Background Notes

I have been driven to write these poems for 12 years. I don't think the urge came from some outside voice, but from inside me, from some burning morsel of personal history and heritage that pushed me constantly to learn all that I could about love.

Much of what's here comes from having the privilege to witness many clients moving through the psychotherapy healing process. Over my decades of therapeutic guiding, I witnessed so many miracles of love and I have felt very humbled and honored every time.

My love education was rounded out by decades of studying and teaching psychology, sociology, counseling and peace studies, as well as studying Buddhism and Sufism and a scattering of other spiritual paths. Lastly, of course, I've learned much through loving and being loved by many people over this life, and from struggling to show compassion, make peace for my part, and learn from my failures.

I've done my best to pull all these strains together in order to put words to some of the thousands of ways that love plays a part in the human journey, as well as what gets in the way of love. I hope these poems challenge and stretch the conceptual boundaries of what we see as love, and debunk some of our limited ideas and myths.

So much literature and art about love focuses on a narrow and superficial view of love-- the kind that is possessive, based on selfish expectations and often fickle if there is trouble. While there are many worthy works out there on the love of parents, friends, and community, there are thousands of fluffy things celebrating idealized romance or unconditional devotion. Few works really look at love's multiple faces and struggles with chaos. Love has to find balance amid a wide array of interactions, massive stupidities, idiotic abuses, and petty put-downs as well as courageous trust, forgiveness and generosity.

Interpersonal Systems Theory

I am an interpersonal systems thinker by training and by passion. I encountered Systems Theory and Interpersonal Science during my doctoral studies, and they fundamentally shifted my thinking and writing from then on.

Interpersonal science explores how we humans influence each other on many levels and in many roles. Systems Theory looks at the processes of chaos, change, boundaries and flow in life and has been applied to relationships in numerous theories. I have worked to understand how these two bodies of knowledge expand on each other for close to 30 years, and you will see that work in many poems here.

We

I have consciously used a 'we' voice whenever possible in writing these poems, despite knowing that it is grammatically and cognitively challenging. I've done this because I am striving for a wider lens, for interpersonal systems thinking, about how we practice love together. I'm also using we to bring forward the perspective of the common good.

When we do not look at how we create the world together, we lose vision and choice in our lives. We must learn to see that we are in this together, that each of us is not the lone source of meaning in life, and that 'they' are not really separate. Everything that happens in our lives is interconnected with and influence by dozens, if not hundreds, of people, animals and things, and I am trying to push us to become conscious of that broader dimension (the big picture).

The we perspective, however you may love or hate it, forces a shift of perspective. Away from separation, differences, identity. Towards awareness of our unity and common fate.

However, it is not my intention that anyone should ever feel constrained to feel or behave as the masses, or give up individual choice in any way. My hope is that holistic thinking could become a conscious choice, to behave for the benefit of me or we or some combination. Couples make that choice several times every day, and couples who thrive are the ones who value the happiness of both. The world would be a better place if all of us thought about each other's welfare more of the time.

If any of you find a serious error in this difficult form (or the gender-neutral 'they' form I also use), or if you have any other constructive feedback, please write to me and share that information for the betterment of all. There are other verbal deviations that may jar some readers, though some are intentional (stretching), but some may be accidental. It's a hard concentration to hold so many visions together, so consistency may be mixed.

Love's Possibilities

There is so much more needed beyond this to explore and discover how love manifests, and I pray that others will continue this work. I hope these words contribute something new and worthwhile to the understanding of love and its multiple upon multiple expressions. My ultimate hope that this work may help you find, create and savor more love in your lives.

Gratitude

I wish to express my gratitude to my beloved grandmother Marguerite Finn Bennett for her great devotion, Boots Doyle, for her loving therapy work, former bosses Ralph Hammond and Billy Ray Browning for believing in me, the faculty of the University of Missouri Counseling Psychology doctoral program for teaching me about systems and interpersonal theory, many Buddhist teachers (mainly Pema Chodron and Lama Shenpen Drolma) for sharing Buddhist teachings that have transformed my life, and to my Sufi teacher, Sabura Deborah Perry, for her loving energy, feedback and support in writing poetry.

Others who deserve thanks include my parents for all the work that went into making me who I am, and my five siblings for hanging in together positively. Lastly, I wish to thank my clients, students, coworkers and friends, for all the life lessons they offered that I am still digesting.

I have put a lot of work and love into these poems, but I have mixed feelings about publishing them because the world is not kind to older women who speak boldly. Still I had to write this before I die and share it with whoever dares to take a look.

JV Connors, Ph.D.

jvconnors7 at gmail dot com,
Interpersonal Peace Center
Silver City, NM, September, 2019

Quote References

Coelho, Paulo (1988). *The alchemist.* San Francisco: HarperOne.

Dostoevsky, Fyodor (1922). *The brothers Karamazov,* New York: Macmillan.

Freire, Paulo (1974). *Pedagogy of the oppressed.* New York: Penguin.

Fromm, Eric (1956). *The art of loving.* New York: Harper & Brothers.

Gyato, Tenzin, the XIV Dalai Lama (1999). *Ancient Wisdom, Modern World: Ethics for the New Millennium.* New York: Little, Brown and Company.

hooks, bell (2000). *All about love: New visions.* New York: William Morrow & Company.

King, Martin L. (1986). *A testament of hope: The essential writings of Martin Luther King, Jr.,* San Francisco: Harper & Row.

von Jacquin, Nikolaus (1787). (entry in Mozart's souvenir album) from Wikipedia.

Robbins, Tim (1980). *Still life with woodpecker.* Basingstoke, Hampshire, England: Sidgwick & Jackson Ltd.

Rumi, Maulana Jalal al-Din, translator: Khalili, Nader, (2001). *Rumi: Dancing the flame.*

Hesperia, CA: Cal-Earth Press.

Shakespeare, William (1602). *Hamlet.*

Williams, Miller (1997). *The ways we touch.* Champaign, IL, University of Illinois Press.

*It is in the shelter of each other that the
people live.*
Irish proverb

Made in the USA
Monee, IL
29 June 2020